Light & Healthy

Light & Healthy

Bounty
Books

First published in Great Britain in 2000 by Hamlyn, a division of Octopus Publishing Group Ltd

This edition published in 2007 by Bounty Books, a division of Octopus Publishing Group Ltd
2–4 Heron Quays, London E14 4JP
Reprinted 2008 (twice)
An Hachette Livre UK Company

ISBN: 978-0-753716-23-6

A CIP catalogue record for this book is available from the British Library

Printed and bound in China

Notes

1 Standard level spoon measurements are used in all recipes.

1 tablespoon = one 15 ml spoon
1 teaspoon = one 5 ml spoon

2 Both imperial and metric measurements have been given in all recipes. Use one set of measurements only and not a mixture of both.

3 Measurements for canned food have been given as a standard metric equivalent.

4 Eggs should be medium unless otherwise stated. The Department of Health advises that eggs should not be consumed raw. This book may contain dishes made with lightly cooked eggs. It is prudent for more vulnerable people, such as pregnant and nursing mothers, invalids, the elderly, babies and young children, to avoid uncooked or lightly cooked dishes made with eggs. Once prepared, these dishes should be used immediately.

5 Poultry should be cooked thoroughly. To test if poultry is cooked, pierce the flesh through the thickest part with a skewer or fork – the juices should run clear, never pink or red.

6 Fresh herbs should be used unless otherwise stated. If unavailable, use dried herbs as an alternative but halve the quantities stated.

7 Pepper should be freshly ground black pepper unless otherwise stated; season according to taste.

8 Ovens should be preheated to the specified temperature – if using a fan-assisted oven, follow the manufacturer's instructions for adjusting the time and the temperature.

9 Do not re-freeze a dish that has been frozen previously.

10 This book includes dishes made with nuts and nut derivatives. It is advisable for customers with known allergic reactions to nuts and nut derivatives and those who may be potentially vulnerable to these allergies, such as pregnant and nursing mothers, invalids, the elderly, babies and children, to avoid dishes made with nuts and nut oils. It is also prudent to check the labels of pre-prepared ingredients for the possible inclusion of nut derivatives.

11 Vegetarians should look for the 'V' symbol on a cheese to ensure it is made with vegetarian rennet. There are vegetarian forms of Parmesan, feta, Cheddar, Cheshire, red Leicester, dolcelatte and many goats' cheeses, among others.

12 All recipes in this book have been analysed by a professional nutritionist, so that you can see their nutritional content at a glance.

The abbreviations are as follows:
kcal = calories;
kj = kilojoules;
CHO = carbohydrate.

The analysis refers to each portion.
Ingredients given as optional are not included in the analysis.

contents

introduction

Food that is light and healthy is a pleasure to eat; it is satisfying without being heavy or cloying, and tasty but not too rich or creamy. The key to a healthy way of eating is to cut back on fats, while making the most of healthy low-fat foods such as fruits, vegetables, grains and pulses.

Nutritionists say that in a 2000 calorie per day diet, no more than 700 calories should come from fat (this means 80 g of fat per day or 40 g on a 1000 calorie diet). A certain amount of fat is essential in the diet but too much saturated fat, found especially in dairy foods, is harmful whereas monounsaturated fat, found in olive oil, and polyunsaturated fats, contained in oily fish such as tuna and mackerel, are beneficial to the heart and circulation system.

Fortunately, there are now various low-fat dairy products on the market. Buy skimmed and semi-skimmed milk rather than whole milk, use low-fat crème fraîche, low-fat yogurt and virtually fat-free fromage frais where possible instead of cream and make use of Quark, full-fat soft cheese (lower in fat than cream cheese) and cottage cheese in cooking.

Choose lean cuts of meat, trying to limit the size of portions to 75 g (3 oz) and cutting off all the visible fat and skin before cooking. Chicken and turkey are considerably lower in fat than most other meats, and white fish is low in fat and high in protein and therefore ideal in a low-fat diet.

Adopting low-fat cooking techniques such as poaching, steaming, stir-frying and griddling helps to reduce your fat intake, particularly if you make a point of using nonstick saucepans, frying pans and woks. Using a low-fat spray oil, available from supermarkets, instead of spooning fat into a pan, also helps to cut back even further on oil consumption.

Another way to cut back on your fat consumption is to avoid processed foods as much as possible. This means turning your back on foods such as crisps, ice cream, sausages, mayonnaise, biscuits and cakes.

The recipes in this book have been analysed by a professional nutritionist so that you can see the calorie and kilojoule count, the protein, carbohydrate (CHO) and fat content of a single serving of each recipe and plan your cooking accordingly: 10–16 g represents a moderate fat content, 5–9 g a low fat content and 4 g or less a very low fat content, so if you choose a main course with a fat content of 4 g or less you can treat yourself to a higher fat dessert. Optional ingredients and serving suggestions, such as a sprinkling of Parmesan cheese, have not been included in the calculations. Not all the recipes are low-fat ones but they have all been selected for their fresh, wholesome and healthy ingredients.

Home-made stocks taste better than any shop-bought version (although some of the new fresh stocks available in the chiller cabinets at supermarkets are very good), and they have the advantage that you know exactly what has gone into them. The three stocks on pages 8 and 9 are all low in fat, and if you make a point of blotting the fat with kitchen paper, the fat content is reduced almost to nothing.

'Another good reducing exercise
consists in placing both hands against
the table edge and pushing back.'
Robert Quillen

french dressing

Combine the vinegar, garlic, mustard and sugar in a small bowl. Add salt and pepper and stir well. Gradually whisk in the olive oil. Taste and add more salt and pepper if necessary. Alternatively, put all the ingredients into a screw-top jar, close the lid tightly and shake well.

2 tablespoons white wine vinegar

1–2 garlic cloves, crushed

2 teaspoons Dijon mustard

¼ teaspoon caster sugar

6 tablespoons extra virgin olive oil

salt and pepper

Makes about 150 ml (¼ pint)

chicken stock

Put the chicken into a large saucepan with the water and bring slowly to the boil, skimming any scum from the surface. Add the bouquet garni, onion, tarragon and salt and pepper to taste. Lower the heat and simmer gently for 1½ hours, skimming regularly. Strain the stock through fine muslin or a very fine strainer. Cool quickly and chill until required.

1.5 kg (3 lb) chicken

2.5 litres (4 pints) water

1 bouquet garni

1 small onion, peeled and stuck with 3 cloves

1 small bunch of tarragon

salt and pepper

Makes 1 litre (1¾ pints)

vegetable stock

Put all the ingredients, except the salt and pepper, in a large saucepan. Bring to the boil slowly, skimming off any surface scum. Add salt and pepper to taste, cover the pan and simmer for about 1½ hours, skimming 3–4 times during cooking. Let the stock cool slightly, then strain through clean muslin or a very fine sieve. Cool quickly, then store in the refrigerator until required.

3 potatoes, peeled and chopped

1 onion, thinly sliced

2 leeks, split and chopped

2 celery sticks, chopped

2 carrots, chopped

1 small fennel head, thinly sliced

thyme sprigs

parsley stalks

2 bay leaves

1.5 litres (2½ pints) water

salt and pepper

Makes 1 litre (1¾ pints)

fish stock

Put all the ingredients, except the wine and salt and pepper, into a large saucepan. Bring slowly to the boil, skimming any scum from the surface. Add the wine and salt and pepper to taste and simmer gently for 30 minutes, skimming once or twice during cooking. Strain the stock through clean muslin or a fine sieve, cool quickly and store in the refrigerator until required.

1 kg (2 lb) fish trimmings

1 small onion, finely chopped

2 leeks, split and chopped

1 bay leaf

parsley stalks

fennel sprigs

lemon rind

1.2 litres (2 pints) water

200 ml (7 fl oz) dry white wine

salt and pepper

Makes 1 litre (1¾ pints)

gazpacho ●

yellow pepper soup ●

chilled pea soup ●

minestrone ●

prawns in ginger sauce ●

grilled mussels with tomatoes & peppers ●

scallops with dill & lime ●

smoked salmon puffs ●

fish terrine ●

tagliatelle romana ●

chicken liver pâté ●

mozzarella salad ●

spinach, mushroom & hazelnut salad ●

waldorf salad ●

soups & starters

gazpacho

1   Combine the garlic and salt in a mortar and pound with a pestle until smooth. Alternatively, place the garlic and salt on a board and crush the garlic with the flattened blade of a knife. Place the bread in a bowl and cover it with cold water. Soak for a few seconds, then drain the bread, squeezing out the moisture.

2   Set aside a quarter of the tomatoes, onions, cucumber and peppers for the garnish. Place the remaining vegetables in a food processor or blender. Add the garlic, bread and oil and process until the mixture is very smooth. Pour the mixture into a bowl and stir in the vinegar and water and pepper to taste. Cover with clingfilm and chill in the refrigerator for at least 3 hours.

3   Serve the soup very cold, garnished with diced avocado, herbs and croûtons, if liked. Chop the reserved vegetables very finely and serve them separately in small bowls.

■ To make croûtons, use 50 g (2 oz) white bread. Cut it into thick slices, cut off the crusts and slice the bread into small squares. Heat 2 tablespoons of oil and fry the croûtons, stirring and tossing until done.

1 garlic clove, roughly chopped

¼ teaspoon salt

3 thick slices of white bread, crusts removed

1 kg (2 lb) tomatoes, skinned and roughly chopped

2 onions, roughly chopped

½ large cucumber, peeled, deseeded and roughly chopped

3 large green peppers, skinned, deseeded and roughly chopped

5 tablespoons olive oil

4 tablespoons white wine vinegar

1 litre (1¾ pints) water

pepper

To Garnish:

75 g (3 oz) avocado, diced

2 tablespoons chopped mixed herbs

croûtons (see below)

Serves 6

Preparation time: 20–30 minutes, plus chilling

kcal 152; kJ 637; **protein** 4 g; **fat** 9 g; CHO 16 g

1   Chop one pepper finely and put it into a small saucepan, then roughly chop the remaining peppers. Melt 25 g (1 oz) of the butter or margarine in another saucepan and cook the onion and roughly chopped peppers for 5 minutes, stirring frequently. Stir in the stock, curry powder, turmeric and coriander, then add the potatoes. Bring to the boil, then lower the heat and simmer, partially covered, for 40–45 minutes, or until the vegetables are soft.

2   Melt the remaining butter with the finely chopped pepper in the small pan and cook over a gentle heat until the pepper is very soft. Reserve for the garnish.

3   Purée the onion, pepper and potato mixture in batches in a food processor or blender until very smooth. Return to a clean saucepan and reheat gently. Serve the soup in warmed soup plates or bowls, garnished with a little of the sautéed chopped pepper.

3 yellow peppers, cored and deseeded

50 g (2 oz) butter or margarine

1 small onion, chopped

1.2 litres (2 pints) Vegetable Stock (see page 9)

1 teaspoon mild curry powder

¼ teaspoon turmeric

1 tablespoon chopped coriander leaves

300 g (10 oz) potatoes, chopped

salt

Serves 8

Preparation time: 15–20 minutes

Cooking time: 50–55 minutes

kcal 90; kJ 376; protein 2 g; fat 5 g; CHO 10 g

yellow pepper soup

■ Slightly sweet, yellow peppers are milder in flavour than green ones. All peppers are rich in vitamin C.

chilled pea soup

1 Place the peas in a large saucepan with the potatoes, onion, mint sprig, lemon rind and juice and stock and season with salt and pepper. Simmer covered for 15–20 minutes or until the peas are tender.

2 Purée in a food processor or blender or press through a sieve. Set aside to cool.

3 Taste and adjust the seasoning then chill in the refrigerator for 2–3 hours. Serve the soup cold, sprinkled with the chopped mint.

375 g (12 oz) freshly shelled peas or frozen petit pois

250 g (8 oz) potatoes, chopped

1 onion, chopped

1 large mint sprig

finely grated rind of ½ lemon

2 tablespoons lemon juice

900 ml (1½ pints) Chicken Stock (see page 8)

salt and pepper

1 tablespoon chopped mint, to garnish

Serves 4

Preparation time: 15 minutes, plus chilling

Cooking time: 20–25 minutes

kcal 100; **kJ** 425; **protein** 6 g; **fat** 1 g; **CHO** 18 g

minestrone

1 Drain the beans and rinse under cold running water.

2 Heat the oil in a large saucepan and add the onions and garlic. Sauté gently for about 5 minutes, stirring occasionally, until soft and golden brown. Add the beans, water, herbs and tomatoes, cover the pan and simmer gently for 2 hours. Add the carrots and simmer for 10 minutes. Stir in the potatoes and turnip and cook for a further 10 minutes.

3 Add the celery and cabbage to the soup with the pasta shapes and cook for 10 minutes, or until the pasta and all the vegetables are tender. Add the parsley and season to taste with salt and pepper. Stir in the Parmesan then ladle the soup into warmed individual soup bowls. Serve immediately with extra Parmesan cheese.

125 g (4 oz) haricot beans, soaked overnight

1 tablespoon vegetable oil

2 onions, chopped

2 garlic cloves, crushed

1.8 litres (3 pints) water

1 teaspoon chopped marjoram

½ teaspoon chopped thyme

4 tomatoes, skinned, deseeded and chopped

2 carrots, diced

2 potatoes, diced

1 small turnip, diced

1–2 celery sticks, chopped

250 g (8 oz) cabbage, shredded

50 g (2 oz) small pasta shapes

1 tablespoon chopped parsley

salt and pepper

3 tablespoons freshly grated Parmesan cheese, plus extra to serve

Serves 8

Preparation time: 20 minutes, plus soaking

Cooking time: about 2½ hours

kcal 157; **kJ** 663; **protein** 8 g; **fat** 3 g; **CHO** 26 g

8 spring onions, chopped

5 cm (2 inch) piece of fresh root ginger, peeled and finely chopped

2 tablespoons dry sherry

2 tablespoons soy sauce

150 ml (¼ pint) Chicken Stock (see page 8)

12 Mediterranean prawns, peeled

salt and pepper

rice or noodles, to serve

1 Place all the ingredients, except the prawns, in a saucepan, and season to taste with salt and pepper.

2 Bring the sauce to the boil, then simmer for 2 minutes. Stir in the prawns, cover and cook for a further 3 minutes. Serve immediately, with rice or noodles.

Serves 4

Preparation time: 10 minutes

Cooking time: about 6 minutes

kcal 50; kJ 214; protein 8 g; fat 1 g; CHO 1 g

prawns in ginger sauce

1 Discard any mussels that are broken or do not shut immediately when tapped sharply with a knife. Put the rest into a large saucepan with the wine, cover, and bring to the boil. Cook over a moderate heat for a few minutes, shaking the pan occasionally until the mussels open. Throw away any mussels that do not open. Remove the open mussels from the pan and discard the top half of each shell.

2 Mix together the chopped pepper, garlic, parsley, tomatoes and 4 tablespoons of the breadcrumbs in a bowl. Stir in 1 tablespoon of the olive oil and season to taste with salt and pepper.

3 Add a little of the mixture to each of the mussels in their shells and place them in an ovenproof dish. Sprinkle with grated Parmesan and the remaining breadcrumbs and olive oil and bake in a preheated oven, 230°C (450°F), Gas Mark 8, for 10 minutes. Then, for a crisp finish, flash the mussels under a preheated hot grill. Sprinkle with parsley and serve immediately.

2.5 litres (4 pints) mussels, scrubbed and debearded

200 ml (7 fl oz) white wine

½ red pepper, cored, deseeded and chopped

2 garlic cloves, crushed

4 tablespoons finely chopped parsley

400 g (13 oz) can chopped tomatoes

5 tablespoons fresh white breadcrumbs

2 tablespoons olive oil

1 tablespoon freshly grated Parmesan cheese

salt and pepper

finely chopped parsley, to garnish

Serves 4
Preparation time: 30 minutes
Cooking time: 20 minutes
kcal 267; **kJ** 1123; **protein** 30 g; **fat** 11 g; **CHO** 14 g

grilled mussels with tomatoes & peppers

juice of 2 limes

375 g (12 oz) scallops

2 tablespoons chopped dill

1 tablespoon chopped mint

¼ cucumber, diced

2 teaspoons sunflower oil

salt and pepper

wholemeal toast, to serve

To Garnish:

lime slices

mint sprigs

Serves 4
Preparation time: 5–10 minutes, plus chilling
Cooking time: 2–3 minutes
kcal 122; **kJ** 515; **protein** 21 g; **fat** 3 g; **CHO** 4 g

1 Pour the lime juice into a saucepan, add the scallops and salt and pepper to taste. Bring the mixture to the boil, then simmer for 2–3 minutes, until the scallops are white in appearance.

2 Remove the pan from the heat and leave to cool. Add the dill, mint, cucumber and oil and turn into a serving dish. Cover and chill for 2 hours to allow the flavours to develop.

3 Garnish the scallops with lime slices and mint sprigs and serve with hot wholemeal toast.

scallops with dill & lime

■ Scallops should be cooked slowly and gently and for just long enough to turn the flesh white. Take care not to overcook them or they will lose their soft, melting texture.

smoked salmon puffs

1 First make the choux pastry. Put the butter and water in a saucepan and bring to the boil. Remove from the heat and immediately beat in the plain and wholemeal flours and cayenne pepper until the dough leaves the side of the pan. Let the mixture cool slightly, then gradually beat in the eggs, a little at a time, until the dough mixture is thoroughly blended.

2 Place teaspoonfuls of the dough on a lightly greased baking sheet, or alternatively pipe the dough, and bake in a preheated oven, 200°C (400°F), Gas Mark 6, for about 20 minutes until well risen and firm to touch. Transfer the choux puffs to a wire rack to cool and split them open to allow the steam to escape.

3 Meanwhile, combine the soured cream and tomato purée to make a dressing. Season to taste with pepper.

4 Cut the smoked salmon into small strips. Fill each puff with a little dressing, and top with some of the fish. Serve with a dusting of cayenne and garnish with mixed salad leaves.

2 tablespoons soured cream
1 teaspoon tomato purée
125–175 g (4–6 oz) smoked salmon
cayenne pepper, for dusting
pepper
mixed salad leaves, to garnish

Choux Pastry:
50 g (2 oz) butter
150 ml (¼ pint) water
25 g (1 oz) plain flour
25 g (1 oz) wholemeal flour
¼ teaspoon cayenne pepper
2 eggs, beaten

Makes about 18

Preparation time: 20 minutes

Cooking time: about 25 minutes

kcal 54; kJ 223; **protein** 3 g; **fat** 4 g; **CHO** 2 g per puff

fish terrine

1 Place the fish fillets in a shallow pan with the wine, bouquet garni, lemon rind and just enough water to cover the fish. Poach, covered, over a gentle heat for 8–10 minutes until the fillets are just tender. Remove the fish with a slotted spoon, then flake and cool. Reserve the cooking liquid.

2 Soften the two cheeses and beat together in a large bowl until smooth. Place 4 tablespoons of the hot fish liquid in a small bowl and sprinkle the gelatine over it. Stir until the gelatine has dissolved. Leave to cool completely, then stir into the cheese mixture.

3 Whisk the egg whites until stiff and fold into the cheese mixture. Divide the mixture in half. Gently stir the cooked fish, lemon juice, chives and pepper into one half. Pour the mixture into a wetted 1 kg (2 lb) loaf tin and chill until set. Stir the prawns, tomato purée and Tabasco sauce into the remaining cheese mixture. Pour on to the fish mixture in the tin and chill until set. If you are not planning to serve the terrine immediately after it has set, cover and refrigerate.

4 To turn out the terrine, dip the loaf tin into a bowl of hot water for a few seconds, then invert on to a dish. Serve the terrine in slices, garnished with dill sprigs.

375 g (12 oz) haddock, whiting or sole fillets, skinned

150 ml (¼ pint) dry white wine

1 bouquet garni

a few strips of pared lemon rind

250 g (8 oz) low-fat cottage cheese

250 g (8 oz) curd or medium fat soft cheese

2 tablespoons gelatine

3 egg whites

1 tablespoon lemon juice

3 tablespoons snipped chives

250 g (8 oz) cooked peeled prawns, roughly chopped

2 tablespoons tomato purée

a few drops of Tabasco sauce

pepper

dill sprigs, to garnish

Serves 6

Preparation time: 45 minutes, plus chilling

Cooking time: 8–10 minutes

kcal 230; **kJ** 970; **protein** 33 g; **fat** 8 g; **CHO** 4 g

1.5 litres (2½ pints) Chicken Stock (see page 8)

250 g (8 oz) tagliatelle

125 g (4 oz) Quark cheese

1 garlic clove, crushed

50 g (2 oz) smoked prosciutto, fat removed and cut into strips

salt and pepper

finely chopped parsley, to garnish

1 Put the chicken stock into a large saucepan and bring to the boil. Add the tagliatelle, stir and cook for 10–12 minutes until just tender, then drain and turn into a hot serving dish.

2 Sieve the Quark and mix in the garlic and seasoning. Stir the cheese mixture into the tagliatelle, toss in the strips of prosciutto, garnish with parsley and serve immediately.

Serves 4
Preparation time: 30 minutes
Cooking time: 10–12 minutes

kcal 258; **kJ** 1096; **protein** 16 g; **fat** 2 g; **CHO** 48 g

tagliatelle romana

chicken liver pâté

1 Heat the butter in a frying pan. Add the onion and fry gently until soft. Add the chicken livers, garlic and salt and pepper to taste and cook until the livers are sealed on the outside but still pink in the centre. Tip the liver mixture into a bowl and chop finely, using 2 sharp knives in a criss-cross manner.

2 Separate the hard-boiled egg whites from the yolks. Chop the egg whites finely and stir them into the liver. Push the egg yolks through a sieve and reserve. (For a smoother texture, the liver mixture and egg whites can be puréed in a food processor or blender.)

3 Cover the pâté and chill for 1–2 hours. Garnish with the sieved egg yolks and serve with triangles of hot toast.

25 g (1 oz) butter

1 small onion, finely chopped

175 g (6 oz) chicken livers, trimmed and chopped

1 garlic clove, crushed

2 hard-boiled eggs

salt and pepper

hot toast, to serve

Serves 4

Preparation time: 10–15 minutes, plus chilling

Cooking time: 4–5 minutes

---

kcal 148; kJ 616; **protein** 12 g; **fat** 11 g; **CHO** 2 g

3 large tomatoes

¼ cucumber

1 red and 1 green pepper, cored and deseeded

2–3 courgettes

250 g (8 oz) mozzarella cheese

4 spring onions, chopped

basil sprigs, to garnish

Dressing:

3 tablespoons olive oil

3–4 tablespoons lime juice

1–2 garlic cloves, crushed

1 teaspoon each clear honey and French mustard

1 tablespoon each chopped parsley, basil and marjoram

1–2 teaspoons green peppercorns

salt

Serves 6

Preparation time: 15 minutes, plus chilling

---

kcal 212; **kJ** 882; **protein** 12 g; **fat** 15 g; **CHO** 8 g

1 Thinly slice the tomatoes, cucumber, peppers, courgettes and mozzarella and arrange them on a serving platter. Sprinkle with the spring onions.

2 To make the dressing, mix together all the ingredients, and season to taste with salt. Spoon the dressing over the salad, then cover and chill for 30 minutes.

3 Remove the salad from the refrigerator 15 minutes before serving and garnish with basil sprigs.

mozzarella salad

175 g (6 oz) young fresh spinach leaves, washed and shaken

125 g (4 oz) button mushrooms, thinly sliced

25 g (1 oz) hazelnuts, chopped

1 To make the dressing, put the olive oil, vinegar, garlic, parsley, yogurt, and salt and pepper to taste in a food processor or blender and processs until smooth.

2 Tear the spinach leaves into pieces and place them in a salad bowl.

3 Add the sliced mushrooms and hazelnuts and toss together. Spoon in the dressing and toss again to blend thoroughly. Alternatively, serve the dressing separately.

Dressing:

2 teaspoons olive oil

2 tablespoons white wine vinegar

1 garlic clove, chopped

2 tablespoons chopped parsley

3 tablespoons natural yogurt

salt and pepper

Serves 6

Preparation time: 15 minutes

kcal 57; **kJ** 238; **protein** 3 g; **fat** 4 g; **CHO** 3 g

spinach, mushroom & hazelnut salad

waldorf salad

1 Mix the apples, celery, grapes and walnuts or pecan nuts with the mayonnaise, stirring so all the ingredients are thoroughly coated with mayonnaise.

2 Spoon the salad into a bowl and arrange a few celery leaves around the edge as a garnish.

4 red dessert apples, cored and diced

1 small head of celery, finely diced, some leaves reserved for garnish

small bunch of seedless grapes, halved

50 g (2 oz) walnuts or pecan nuts, coarsely chopped

50 ml (2 fl oz) low-fat mayonnaise

Serves 6
Preparation time: 15–20 minutes
kcal 127; **kJ** 530; **protein** 2 g; **fat** 8 g; **CHO** 12 g

bitter leaf salad with toasted nuts & seeds ●

fusilli salad with asparagus, peas & lemon ●

creole okra rice ●

mediterranean vegetables with fresh herbs ●

spinach & ricotta gnocchi ●

spaghetti with mushrooms & herbs ●

tomato tagliatelle ●

pasta shells with bacon & broccoli ●

chicken with garlic noodles ●

chicken & pepper kebabs ●

duck with ginger & sesame seeds ●

seafood brochettes marinated in lime juice ●

light dishes

bitter leaf salad with toasted nuts & seeds

1 Arrange the nuts and seeds in a single layer on a large baking sheet. Place under a preheated moderately hot grill and toast for 2–3 minutes, turning frequently until they are lightly browned. Transfer the mixture to a plate and leave to cool.

2 Tear the radicchio and frisée leaves into bite-sized pieces and place in a large salad bowl. Add the chicory and onion and salt and pepper to taste. Toss the salad leaves lightly to mix evenly.

3 Spoon the dressing over the leaves and sprinkle the salad with the toasted nuts and seeds.

■ To make a yogurt dressing, mix 150 ml (¼ pint) natural yogurt with 1 tablespoon lemon juice, 1 teaspoon clear honey, ½ teaspoon Dijon mustard and salt and pepper and beat until smooth. Vary the dressing by adding extra flavourings, such as curry paste or finely grated orange rind.

25 g (1 oz) flaked almonds

25 g (1 oz) pine nuts

2 tablespoons sunflower seeds

1 small head of radicchio, separated into leaves

1 small head of of frisée, separated into leaves

1 head of chicory, separated into leaves

1 mild onion, thinly sliced

1 quantity Yogurt Dressing (see below)

salt and pepper

Serves 6
Preparation time: 10 minutes
Cooking time: 2–3 minutes
kcal 301; kJ 1264; **protein** 14 g; **fat** 12 g; **CHO** 39 g

fusilli salad with asparagus, peas & lemon

1 Cook the pasta in a large saucepan of lightly salted boiling water for 10–12 minutes or according to packet instructions until just tender. Drain in a colander and rinse under cold running water. Drain thoroughly and transfer to a serving bowl.

2 Cook the asparagus in a shallow saucepan of boiling water for 4–5 minutes, until almost tender. Drain in a colander, cool under cold running water, then drain again thoroughly. Add to the pasta.

3 Add the peas, tomatoes, basil and parsley to the pasta. Using a zester, remove the rind from the lemon in thin narrow strips and add these to the salad. Season well with salt and pepper.

4 Just before serving squeeze the juice from the lemon and add it to the salad with the French dressing. Toss lightly.

Long fusilli – twisted lengths of pasta – are attractively shaped, rather like curly spaghetti, but you could also use short pasta shapes such as penne, quills, or farfalle (bows), if you prefer.

250 g (8 oz) dried long fusilli

375 g (12 oz) asparagus spears, trimmed and cut into 5 cm (2 inch) lengths

125 g (4 oz) frozen peas, thawed

2 large tomatoes, skinned, deseeded and chopped

small handful of basil leaves, torn

small handful of parsley leaves, torn

1 small lemon

1 quantity French Dressing (see page 8)

salt and pepper

Serves 4
Preparation time: 15 minutes
Cooking time: about 15 minutes

kcal 368; **kJ** 1549; **protein** 13 g; **fat** 13 g; **CHO** 53 g

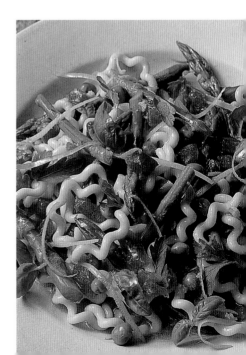

creole okra rice

1 Heat the oil in a large saucepan, add the rice and fry for 2 minutes. Add the stock, salt, chillies and red pepper, stirring well, and bring to the boil. Lower the heat, cover the pan and simmer for 5 minutes.

2 Add the okra, replace the lid and continue to simmer for about 12 minutes, or until the rice has absorbed all the stock and is tender but still firm.

3 Transfer the mixture to a warmed serving dish, season with pepper to taste and serve immediately.

2 tablespoons corn oil

500 g (1 lb) long-grain rice

600 ml (1 pint) Chicken Stock (see page 8) or Vegetable Stock (see page 9)

½ teaspoon salt

2 chillies, deseeded and cut into fine strips

1 red pepper, cored, deseeded and chopped

275 g (9 oz) okra, stems trimmed

pepper

Serves 4

Preparation time: 10–15 minutes

Cooking time: about 20 minutes

kcal 533; **kJ** 2225; **protein** 12 g; **fat** 7 g; **CHO** 104 g

mediterranean vegetables with fresh herbs

1 Heat the oil in a saucepan, add the garlic and onions and fry very gently for 10 minutes, stirring occasionally.

2 Add the green peppers and cook gently, stirring, for 1 minute. Add the tomatoes and their juice, then the parsley, basil and thyme and salt and pepper to taste. Bring to the boil, then lower the heat, cover and simmer for 30 minutes, stirring occasionally until the vegetables are very soft. Remove the pan from the heat.

3 Stir in the capers and black olives, then taste and adjust the seasoning. Serve warm or chilled.

3 tablespoons olive oil

1 garlic clove, crushed

3 large onions, sliced

3 large green peppers, cored, deseeded and sliced

400 g (13 oz) can tomatoes

3 tablespoons chopped parsley

2 tablespoons chopped basil

2 tablespoons chopped thyme

1–2 tablespoons capers

10–12 black olives, pitted

salt and pepper

Serves 4

Preparation time: 20 minutes

Cooking time: 45 minutes

kcal 190; kJ 795; protein 5 g; fat 11 g; CHO 21 g

■ This is a simple variation of the French vegetable dish ratatouille and may be served chilled in individual serving dishes as a light summer meal. The many herbs give it a rich flavour. Red peppers may be used instead of the green ones.

spinach & ricotta gnocchi

1 Remove the stalks from the spinach, then wash but do not dry the leaves. Chop them and heat in a saucepan until they wilt and any visible liquid has disappeared. Tip into a sieve and squeeze out as much liquid as possible – this is very important. Return the spinach to the pan, add the flour, if using, and heat gently, stirring, to complete the drying. Remove from the heat, beat in the egg and mix in the ricotta and Parmesan, nutmeg and salt and pepper.

2 Break off small balls of the mixture and roll lightly in seasoned flour. To shape the gnocchi, hold a fork in one hand, take a piece of pasta in the other and press it lightly against the inner curve of the prongs. Then, with a quick downward movement, flip it towards the end of the prongs so it is concave on one side, and convex and ridged on the other. Chill the gnocchi for about 1 hour.

3 Half fill a large frying pan with water and bring to simmering point, then lower in some of the gnocchi, but do not crowd the pan. Poach until they rise to the surface, then transfer to a warmed plate with a slotted spoon. Cook the remaining gnocchi in the same way. Serve warm with melted butter and Parmesan.

1 kg (2 lb) fresh spinach

about 2 tablespoons plain flour (optional)

1 large egg, beaten

250 g (8 oz) fresh ricotta cheese

50 g (2 oz) Parmesan cheese, grated

pinch of freshly grated nutmeg

seasoned plain flour, for coating

salt and pepper

To Serve:

melted unsalted butter

Parmesan shavings

Serves 4
Preparation time: 45 minutes, plus chilling
Cooking time: 8 minutes, plus cooking the gnocchi
kcal 268; kJ 1119; protein 22 g; fat 14 g CHO 18 g

1. Heat the oil in a saucepan, add the onion and garlic and fry gently for 2–3 minutes.

2. Add the mushrooms, then the herbs and season with salt and pepper. Continue to fry gently for a few minutes until the mushrooms have softened and darkened, then add the white wine and simmer for about 5 minutes.

3. Meanwhile, bring a large saucepan of salted water to the boil. Add the pasta, stir and cook for 10–12 minutes until tender.

4. Drain the pasta and pile into a warmed serving dish. Toss with the sauce and serve immediately.

2 teaspoons olive oil

75 g (3 oz) onion, finely sliced

1 garlic clove, crushed

175 g (6 oz) mushrooms, finely sliced

1 tablespoon mixed herbs

1 teaspoon dried sage, oregano or thyme

2 tablespoons white wine

200 g (7 oz) spaghetti

salt and pepper

Serves 2
Preparation time: 8–10 minutes
Cooking time: 10–12 minutes
kcal 404; **kJ** 1715; **protein** 14 g; **fat** 5 g; **CHO** 78 g

spaghetti with mushrooms & herbs

tomato tagliatelle

1 To make the sauce, heat the oil in a saucepan and cook the onions gently for 3 minutes, stirring once or twice. Add the garlic, courgettes and green pepper and cook for 3 minutes. Add the tomatoes and mushrooms, stir well, cover the pan and simmer for 10 minutes, or until the vegetables are just tender. Season with salt and pepper and stir in the parsley.

2 Meanwhile, bring a large saucepan of lightly salted water to the boil, add the pasta, stir and cook for about 5 minutes, or until tender. Drain the pasta, rinse with hot water to stop it becoming sticky, and drain again.

3 Turn the tagliatelle into a warmed serving dish, pour on the sauce and toss well. Garnish with oregano sprigs and serve immediately.

1 tablespoon vegetable oil

2 onions, sliced

2 garlic cloves, crushed

500 g (1 lb) courgettes, thinly sliced

1 green pepper, cored, deseeded and sliced

2 large tomatoes, skinned and chopped

250 g (8 oz) button mushrooms

2 tablespoons chopped parsley

500 g (1 lb) fresh tagliatelle

salt and pepper

oregano sprigs, to garnish

Serves 6

Preparation time: about 20 minutes

Cooking time: 20 minutes

kcal 342; **kJ** 1451; **protein** 13 g; **fat** 4 g; **CHO** 68 g

---

■ To skin tomatoes, first cut a cross in the base. Plunge them in boiling water and leave for 30 seconds, until the skin starts to peel away from the cross. Lift them out with a slotted spoon, let them cool slightly, then peel off the skin.

1 Cook the broccoli in boiling water for 7–8 minutes, until just tender. Drain, refresh under cold running water, then drain again.

2 Cook the pasta in plenty of lightly salted boiling water until just tender or according to packet instructions.

3 Meanwhile, heat the oil in a frying pan, add the bacon and cook, stirring occasionally, until it is lightly browned, adding the garlic towards the end. Add the nuts and heat until lightly toasted. Stir in the broccoli.

4 Drain the pasta, tip into a warmed serving bowl and pour the broccoli mixture over it. Season with salt and pepper. Toss quickly and serve with grated Pecorino cheese.

375 g (12 oz) broccoli florets

375 g (12 oz) pasta shells

1 tablespoon olive oil

50 g (2 oz) lean bacon, diced

2 garlic cloves, sliced

25 g (1 oz) pine nuts

salt and pepper

freshly grated Pecorino cheese, to serve

Serves 4
Preparation time: 10 minutes
Cooking time: about 15 minutes
kcal 438; kJ 1850; protein 19 g; fat 11 g; CHO 71 g

pasta shells with bacon & broccoli

chicken with garlic noodles

1 Heat the oil and half the butter in a saucepan, add the onion and cook for 5 minutes, until transparent. Cut the chicken into 5 cm (2 inch) pieces, add to the pan and brown on all sides. Add the garlic, wine, tarragon, and salt and pepper and bring to the boil. Cover and simmer for 30 minutes. Remove the garlic, stir in the mushrooms and cook for 2 minutes. Stir in the parsley.

2 Meanwhile, cook the pasta until just tender or according to packet instructions. Drain thoroughly and toss with the remaining butter.

3 Mix together the sauce and noodles, spoon into a buttered ovenproof dish, and sprinkle with the breadcrumbs and Parmesan cheese. Bake in a preheated oven, 200°C (400°F), Gas Mark 6, for 20–25 minutes, until hot and golden brown. Garnish with tarragon, and serve immediately.

1 tablespoon oil

25 g (1 oz) butter

1 large onion, chopped

500 g (1 lb) boneless, skinless chicken breasts

2–3 garlic bulbs, separated into cloves

300 ml (½ pint) dry white wine

1 tablespoon chopped tarragon

125 g (4 oz) button mushrooms, sliced

4 tablespoons chopped parsley

500 g (1 lb) fresh noodles or tagliatelle verde

25 g (1 oz) dried wholemeal breadcrumbs

15 g (½ oz) Parmesan cheese, grated

salt and pepper

tarragon sprigs, to garnish

Serves 6

Preparation time: 10 minutes

Cooking time: about 1 hour

kcal 478; kJ 1942; **protein** 31 g; **fat** 11 g; **CHO** 57 g

chicken & pepper kebabs

1 Mix together the yogurt, oil, garlic, coriander and cumin in a shallow dish with salt and pepper to taste. Add the pieces of chicken and stir well. Cover and marinate at room temperature for 30 minutes–1 hour.

2 Thread the pieces of chicken on to presoaked bamboo or oiled metal skewers, alternating them with chunks of onion and red and green pepper.

3 Cook the kebabs under a preheated hot grill, turning frequently, for 20 minutes or until the chicken is tender when pierced with a skewer or fork. Serve hot, on a bed of mixed salad leaves, garnished with lime wedges.

■ Cut the chicken, onion and red pepper into chunks of roughly the same size. This gives the kebabs a neat appearance and helps to ensure even cooking.

150 ml (¼ pint) natural yogurt

2 tablespoons extra virgin olive oil

2 garlic cloves, crushed

2 tablespoons chopped coriander leaves

1 tablespoon ground cumin

8 boneless, skinless chicken thighs, cut into large chunks

1 onion, cut into chunks

1 red pepper, cored, deseeded and cut into chunks

1 green pepper, cored, deseeded and cut into chunks

salt and pepper

To Serve:

mixed salad leaves

lime wedges

Serves 4

Preparation time: 15 minutes, plus marinating

Cooking time: 20 minutes

kcal 237; **kJ** 988; **protein** 23 g; **fat** 12 g; **CHO** 11 g

duck with ginger & sesame seeds

1 Combine the marinade ingredients in a large bowl and add the duck pieces. Cover and marinate for 3–4 hours in a cool place or overnight in the refrigerator. Spoon the marinade over the duck several times during marinating, making sure that you coat the pieces evenly.

2 Remove the duck with a slotted spoon and thread on to 8 bamboo skewers, previously soaked in water, or 4 metal skewers.

3 Place the skewers on the grid of a moderately hot barbecue or under a preheated moderately hot grill and cook the small skewers for 8–10 minutes and the larger ones for 10–12 minutes. Turn the skewers several times during cooking and baste with the remaining marinade.

4 Serve the duck hot or cold, either on or off the skewers.

■ Pre-packed, ready-prepared duck breasts are on sale at the poultry counter of larger supermarkets. They are excellent for stir-fries, or for grilling or barbecuing, as in this recipe.

4 boneless, skinless duck breasts, cut into 32 even-sized pieces

Marinade:

2 tablespoons brown sugar

1 teaspoon salt

4 tablespoons light soy sauce

1 tablespoon sesame oil

1 cm (½ inch) piece of fresh root ginger, peeled and finely chopped

1 teaspoon sesame seeds

Serves 4

Preparation time: 20–25 minutes, plus marinating

Cooking time: 8–12 minutes

kcal 286; **kJ** 1203; **protein** 31 g; **fat** 13 g; **CHO** 12 g

seafood brochettes marinated in lime juice

1 To make the marinade, put the lime juice, olive oil and garlic into a large bowl with salt and pepper and mix thoroughly. Put the prepared seafood into the marinade (cut the scallops in half if they are very large) and stir gently until completely coated. Cover and refrigerate for at least 1 hour.

2 Remove the seafood from the marinade and thread on to wooden or metal skewers. Place the skewers on the rack of a grill pan and brush with the remaining marinade. Grill for about 5 minutes, turning occasionally, until cooked and tender. Baste with more marinade if liked.

3 To make the chilli butter, blend the softened butter with the chopped chillies until they are thoroughly mixed.

4 To serve, arrange the seafood brochettes with a bed of rice and put a pat of chilli butter on top of each one. Scatter with chopped coriander.

juice of 2 limes

2 tablespoons olive oil

2 garlic cloves, crushed

500 g (1 lb) mixed seafood (uncooked prawns, fresh tuna, scallops)

salt and pepper

a few chopped coriander leaves, to garnish

plain boiled rice, to serve

Chilli Butter:

50 g (2 oz) butter, softened

2 hot chillies, chopped (preferably jalapeño)

Serves 4
Preparation time: 20 minutes, plus marinating
Cooking time: 5 minutes

kcal 227; **kJ** 946; **protein** 26 g; **fat** 12 g; **CHO** 3 g

■ Chillies are the most fiery variety of pepper, so take care when cooking with them. The seeds are the hottest part, so remove them if you prefer.

the
main meal

indonesian fish curry

1 Wash the mackerel fillets and pat dry on kitchen paper. Cut each fillet into pieces measuring about 7 x 5 cm (3 x 2 inches). Rub the fillets with ½ teaspoon of the salt and the lemon juice. Set aside.

2 Place the remaining salt, onion, garlic, ginger, turmeric, shrimp paste, sambal oelek, lemon grass and coconut milk in a wide sauté pan. Bring to simmering point, then reduce the heat and cook gently for 15 minutes, until the sauce has thickened slightly. Strain the tamarind pulp through a sieve, pressing it against the side to extract as much juice as possible. Discard the pulp and add the liquid to the sauce. Stir well and cook gently for a further 5 minutes.

3 Add the mackerel and coriander and cook over a low heat for 6–7 minutes, until the fish is cooked. Stir in the grated coconut, cook for 3 minutes, or until the coconut has dissolved. Garnish with coriander sprigs and serve with rice.

500 g (1 lb) mackerel fillets

1 teaspoon salt

juice of ½ lemon

1 large onion, finely chopped

4 garlic cloves, crushed

1 tablespoon grated fresh root ginger

1 teaspoon turmeric

1 teaspoon dried shrimp paste

1 tablespoon sambal oelek (hot pepper condiment)

1 lemon grass stalk, halved lengthways

300 ml (½ pint) coconut milk

1 tablespoon tamarind pulp, soaked in 150 ml (¼ pint) boiling water for 10 minutes

3 tablespoons chopped coriander leaves

25 g (1 oz) creamed coconut, finely grated

coriander sprigs, to garnish

boiled rice, to serve

Serves 6

Preparation time: 20 minutes, plus soaking

Cooking time: 35 minutes

kcal 240; **kJ** 1000; **protein** 17 g; **fat** 17 g; **CHO** 6 g

25 g (1 oz) creamed coconut

150 ml (¼ pint) boiling water

150 ml (¼ pint) Fish Stock
(see page 9)

750 g (1½ lb) monkfish

1 tablespoon oil

6 spring onions, chopped

3 green chillies, deseeded and
chopped

1 red pepper, cored, deseeded and
chopped

1 garlic clove, crushed

5 cm (2 inch) piece of fresh root
ginger, peeled and chopped

½ teaspoon ground cumin

½ teaspoon ground coriander

1 teaspoon grated lemon rind

1 tablespoon lemon juice

1 tablespoon dry sherry

salt and pepper

boiled rice, to serve

To Garnish:

lemon wedges

coriander leaves

1 Place the creamed coconut in a bowl, pour over the boiling water and fish stock and leave to infuse for 30 minutes. Reserve the liquid.

2 Meanwhile, cut the fish into 5 cm (2 inch) cubes. Heat the oil in a large pan, stir in all the remaining ingredients and season with salt and pepper to taste. Add the fish, pour on the coconut milk mixture and bring to the boil, then simmer for 5 minutes.

3 Transfer to a warmed serving dish, garnish with lemon and coriander, and serve with rice.

Serves 4
Preparation time: 15–20 minutes, plus infusing
Cooking time: 5–10 minutes
kcal 212; kJ 893; protein 31 g; fat 8 g; CHO 3 g

creamed coconut monkfish

chinese steamed whole fish

1   Pour cold water into a large wok to come about one-third of the way up the side, then place a large bamboo steamer in the wok, making sure that it does not touch the water. Bring the water to the boil over a moderate heat.

2   Meanwhile, make diagonal slashes on each side of the fish, working right down to the bones. Place the two fish, head to tail on a plate that will just fit inside the steamer. Insert the slices of ginger inside the fish and in the diagonal slashes, then sprinkle about half of the spring onions and garlic inside and over the fish. Drizzle each fish with 1 teaspoon of the sesame oil. Put the plate of fish inside the steamer and cover with a lid. Steam over a high heat for 8 minutes, without lifting the lid.

3   While the fish is cooking, mash about two-thirds of the black beans, leaving the rest whole. Heat the remaining sesame oil and the groundnut oil in a small wok or saucepan. Add the remaining spring onions and garlic, the mashed and whole black beans and the rice wine or sherry and stir-fry over a high heat for a few minutes until sizzling.

4   Transfer the fish to a warmed serving platter. Pour any fish juices from the cooking plate into the sauce, then spoon the sauce over the fish. Serve immediately with noodles and garnished with coriander.

2 whole sea bass or grey mullet, each about 500 g (1 lb), gutted and trimmed, with heads and tails left on

5 cm (2 inch) piece of fresh root ginger, peeled and very thinly sliced

6 spring onions, sliced into very thin rings

4 garlic cloves, finely sliced

3 teaspoons sesame oil

3 heaped tablespoons canned salted black beans, rinsed

1 tablespoon groundnut oil

2 tablespoons rice wine or dry sherry

2–3 tablespoons chopped coriander leaves, to garnish

bean thread noodles, to serve

Serves 2
Preparation time: 20 minutes
Cooking time: about 10 minutes
kcal 308; **kJ** 1290; **protein** 40 g; **fat** 15 g; **CHO** 3 g

■ A whole fish is a symbol of prosperity in China, which is why they are often served at banquets. The head and tail are always left on the fish, and the head should face the guest of honour.

prawn gumbo

1 Bring a large saucepan of lightly salted water to the boil. Add the rice and cook for 8–10 minutes or until tender. Drain the rice and set aside.

2 Melt the butter in a large heavy-based saucepan. Add the garlic and onion and cook gently for about 5 minutes or until soft and slightly golden. Add the red pepper and cook over a moderate heat for a further 5 minutes, stirring constantly.

3 Stir in the tomatoes and cayenne and mix well. Pour in the fish stock and bring the mixture to the boil. Add the okra, lower the heat, cover the pan and cook for 20 minutes, stirring occasionally.

4 Add the prawns, rice and lime juice to the soup. Stir well, cover and simmer for a further 5–8 minutes. Season with salt and pepper and add a little more cayenne, if liked.

50 g (2 oz) white long-grain rice

50 g (2 oz) butter

2 garlic cloves, crushed

1 onion, chopped

1 red pepper, cored, deseeded and finely chopped

4 ripe tomatoes, skinned and chopped

¼ teaspoon cayenne pepper or more to taste

1.2 litres (2 pints) Fish Stock (see page 9)

375 g (12 oz) okra, trimmed and sliced

375 g (12 oz) large prawns, cooked and peeled

1 tablespoon freshly squeezed lime juice

salt and pepper

Serves 6

Preparation time: 20 minutes

Cooking time: 50 minutes

kcal 210; **kJ** 877; **protein** 18 g; **fat** 9 g; **CHO** 16 g

This Cajun soup comes from coast of Louisiana in the south of the United States. It can be made with vegetables, meats and seafood, but okra is its most important ingredient, as it thickens the soup.

625 g (1¼ lb) swordfish, cut into 2.5 x 4 cm (1 x 1½ inch) cubes

oil, for greasing

lemon wedges, to serve

Marinade:

4 tablespoons lemon juice

1 tablespoon olive oil

3 tablespoons finely chopped red onion

2 bay leaves, torn

1½ teaspoons paprika

salt and pepper

Lemon Sauce:

2 tablespoons virgin olive oil

3 tablespoons lemon juice

3 tablespoons chopped parsley

salt and pepper

1 Mix together all the marinade ingredients. Place the swordfish cubes in a single layer in a wide, shallow, non-metallic dish. Pour over the marinade, turning the swordfish so it is evenly coated. Cover and leave in a cool place for 4–5 hours, turning the fish occasionally.

2 Mix together all the lemon sauce ingredients in a jug and set aside. Oil a grill rack.

3 Thread the fish on to 4 skewers and cook under a preheated hot grill or over a hot barbecue for 4–5 minutes on each side, basting frequently with the marinade. Serve with the lemon sauce and lemon wedges.

Serves 4
Preparation time: 15 minutes, plus marinating
Cooking time: 8–10 minutes

kcal 273; **kJ** 1140; **protein** 29 g; **fat** 16 g; **CHO** 3 g

turkish skewered swordfish

chinese chilli chicken

1 Cut the chicken into thin strips, working diagonally against the grain, and place them in a non-metallic dish. Mix together all the marinade ingredients and pour them over the chicken. Cover and leave to marinate at room temperature for about 30 minutes.

2 Heat a wok until hot. Add the oil and heat until hot. Add the ginger, garlic and 1 tablespoon of the chilli sauce and stir-fry over a low heat for 1–2 minutes then add the chicken, increase the heat to high and stir-fry for 3 minutes. Pour in about 200 ml (7 fl oz) of the stock and continue stir-frying for 3 minutes or until the chicken is tender.

3 Lift the chicken out of the sauce with a slotted spoon and place it in a warmed serving dish. Add the remaining stock to the wok, stir, then simmer, stirring occasionally, for about 5 minutes. Blend the cornflour to a paste with a little cold water, pour it into the wok and stir to mix. Simmer, stirring, for 1–2 minutes until the sauce thickens. Stir the coriander into the sauce, then taste and add salt if necessary, plus more chilli sauce if you like. Pour the sauce over the chicken, garnish with chopped chilli and coriander leaves and serve immediately.

2 boneless, skinless chicken breasts, total weight 250–300 g (8–10 oz)

1 tablespoon groundnut oil

2.5 cm (1 inch) piece of fresh root ginger, peeled and crushed

1 garlic clove, crushed

1–2 tablespoons chilli sauce, to taste

450 ml (¾ pint) hot Chicken Stock (see page 8)

1 teaspoon cornflour

1 tablespoon chopped coriander leaves

salt

Marinade:

3 tablespoons dark soy sauce

1 tablespoon rice wine or dry sherry

1 teaspoon sugar

To Garnish:

½ small red chilli, very finely chopped

coriander leaves

Serves 3
Preparation time: 5 minutes, plus marinating
Cooking time: about 12 minutes
kcal 180; **kJ** 759; **protein** 23 g; **fat** 7 g; **CHO** 6 g

■ Bottled Chinese chilli sauce can be found in supermarkets. Brands vary in strength.

chicken tandoori

1 Make incisions in the chicken flesh and rub with the garlic. Place the chicken in a large shallow bowl. Mix the tandoori powder with the yogurt and pour over the chicken. Cover and leave to marinate in the refrigerator for 3 hours.

2 Remove the chicken breasts from the marinade and put them on a grill rack. Place under a preheated moderate grill and grill for about 20 minutes or until the chicken is cooked through, turning frequently and basting with the marinade.

3 Arrange the chicken on a bed of shredded lettuce with the banana slices, onion and lemon wedges and serve immediately.

4 boneless chicken breasts, skinned, each about 175 g (6 oz)

1 garlic clove, crushed

1 tablespoon tandoori powder

300 g (10 oz) natural yogurt

To Serve:

finely shredded lettuce

banana slices, dipped in lemon juice and sprinkled with desiccated coconut

onion slices

lemon wedges

Serves 4

Preparation time: 20 minutes, plus marinating

Cooking time: 20 minutes

kcal 250; **kJ** 1055; **protein** 42 g; **fat** 6 g; **CHO** 6 g

chicken with oyster mushrooms & crème fraîche

1 Fry the strips of bacon gently in a large flameproof casserole, stirring, for about 5 minutes until the fat runs. Add the butter and, when it has melted, add the chicken and sauté over a moderate heat for about 5 minutes until golden on all sides.

2 Sprinkle in the flour and turn the chicken to cover all over, then gradually stir in the wine and bring to the boil, stirring. Add the mushrooms, garlic, crème fraîche, rosemary and plenty of pepper. Stir well, then cover the casserole and simmer gently for 25 minutes or until the chicken is tender when pierced with a skewer or fork, turning and basting it frequently.

3 Taste the sauce for seasoning. Serve each chicken breast sliced and garnished with a sprig of rosemary, an oyster mushroom and some crème fraîche.

125 g (4 oz) smoked streaky bacon rashers, rinded and cut into strips

15 g (½ oz) butter

6 large skinless chicken breasts

1 tablespoon plain flour

300 ml (½ pint) dry white wine

175 g (6 oz) oyster mushrooms, thinly sliced, plus extra to garnish

1 garlic clove, crushed

75 ml (3 fl oz) half-fat crème fraîche, plus extra to serve

½ teaspoon chopped rosemary

salt and pepper

rosemary sprigs, to garnish

Serves 6
Preparation time: 20 minutes
Cooking time: about 40 minutes
kcal 310; **kJ** 1296; **protein** 33 g; **fat** 15 g; **CHO** 4 g

pesto chicken & pepper salad

1 Shred the chicken and set aside. Place the peppers under a hot grill and leave until the skin is charred.

2 When the peppers are cool enough to handle, rub off and discard the charred skin. Slice the flesh into thin strips, and discard the seeds and core. Season with salt and pepper.

3 To make the pesto dressing combine the basil leaves, Parmesan, vinegar, pine nuts and garlic in a food processor or blender. Add pepper to taste. Process for a few seconds. With the motor running, drizzle in the olive oil through the feeder tube until the mixture becomes thick and smooth. Pour into a bowl or jug and use as required.

4 This dressing can also be made using a mortar and pestle. Pound together the basil, pine nuts and garlic to form a thick paste. Add the Parmesan, vinegar, pepper and oil and stir vigorously to mix.

5 Arrange the salad leaves on a serving dish or individual plates. Pile the peppers on to the salad leaves, with the olives and chicken. Spoon the pesto dressing over the chicken mixture. Serve immediately, drizzled with olive oil and garnished with basil sprigs.

6 x 125 g (4 oz) boneless, skinless chicken breasts, cooked

1 red pepper

1 yellow pepper

75 g (3 oz) mixed salad leaves (rocket, frisée, young spinach)

50 g (2 oz) black olives, pitted

1 quantity Pesto Dressing (see below)

1 teaspoon olive oil, to drizzle

salt and pepper

basil sprigs, to garnish

Pesto Dressing:

15 g (½ oz) basil leaves

15 g (½ oz) Parmesan cheese, grated

2 tablespoons white wine vinegar

½ tablespoon pine nuts

½ garlic clove, crushed

50 ml (2 fl oz) extra virgin olive oil

pepper

Serves 6
Preparation time: 15 minutes
Cooking time: 10–15 minutes
kcal 263; kJ 1100; **protein** 30 g; **fat** 15 g; **CHO** 1 g

paella with chicken

1 Heat the oil in a 40 cm (16 inch) paella pan or 4.2 litre (7 pint) wide shallow casserole. Add the chicken and rabbit and cook until lightly browned. Stir in the onion and garlic and fry for 5 minutes, then add the paprika and then the rice. Stir for 2–3 minutes, then stir in the tomatoes with all but 2 tablespoons of the stock, the rosemary and salt and pepper. Dissolve the saffron in the remaining stock, add to the paella and let it boil for 8–10 minutes without stirring.

2 Scatter the green beans and broad beans over the paella – do not stir. Gradually turn down the heat and leave to simmer for about 8–10 minutes until the rice is tender and all the liquid absorbed. Cover the paella with a heavy cloth, remove from the heat and leave to stand for 5–10 minutes before serving.

1 tablespoon olive oil

500 g (1 lb) boneless, skinless chicken breasts

4 small rabbit portions

2 Spanish onions, chopped

4 garlic cloves, chopped

1 tablespoon paprika

375 g (12 oz) paella or risotto rice

3 extra large sun-ripened tomatoes, skinned, deseeded and chopped

1.8 litres (3 pints) boiling Chicken Stock (see page 8)

1 rosemary sprig

large pinch of saffron threads, finely crushed

150 g (5 oz) green beans, cut into short lengths

125 g (4 oz) broad beans

salt and pepper

Serves 4
Preparation time: 20–30 minutes
Cooking time: about 45 minutes
kcal 629; **kJ** 2656; **protein** 32 g; **fat** 15 g; **CHO** 98 g

■ A paella is both a substantial Spanish rice dish and the name of the two-handled pan in which it is cooked. The original paella (the meal) was a country dish from Valencia.

375 g (12 oz) skinless turkey breast fillets, cut into 4 cm (1½ inches) chunks

grated rind and juice of 2 oranges

1 tablespoon cornflour

1 tablespoon sunflower oil

1 teaspoon sesame seed oil

½ red pepper, cored, deseeded and cut into neat strips

½ green pepper, cored, deseeded and cut into neat strips

3 celery sticks, diced

125 g (4 oz) carrots, cut into matchstick slices

salt and pepper

plain boiled rice, to serve

Marinade:

1 tablespoon soy sauce

2 tablespoons orange juice

Serves 4
Preparation time: 25–30 minutes, plus marinating
Cooking time: 12–15 minutes
kcal 189; **kJ** 798; **protein** 21 g; **fat** 5 g; **CHO** 16 g

1 To make the marinade, mix together the soy sauce and orange juice in a bowl. Add the turkey pieces, cover and leave to marinate for 30 minutes.

2 Measure the orange juice and add enough water to make 150 ml (¼ pint). Blend in the cornflour and add a little salt and pepper. Remove the turkey from the marinade and drain well, reserving the marinade.

3 Heat the sunflower and sesame oils in a wok. Add the turkey pieces and stir-fry for 4–5 minutes, then add the orange rind, peppers, celery and carrots and stir-fry for a further 3 minutes.

4 Pour the cornflour and orange juice mixture and the remaining marinade into the wok and bring to the boil, stirring until slightly thickened. Serve with plain boiled rice.

turkey & orange stir-fry with mixed vegetables

1 Boil the carrots in lightly salted boiling water for 10 minutes. Add the leek and cook for a further 5–8 minutes. The vegetables should retain a slight 'bite'. Drain and refresh under cold water. Drain again and set aside.

2 Melt the butter in a large saucepan over a moderate heat. Add the onion and cook until soft but not browned. Add the flour and cook, stirring, for 2 minutes. Remove from the heat and gradually stir in the stock and reserved can juices. Return to the heat and cook, stirring constantly, until the sauce has thickened and is almost boiling. Season to taste with salt and pepper. Add the cooked turkey and mix well. Transfer the mixture to a buttered ovenproof dish and set aside.

3 To make the topping, place the flour in a bowl. Add the butter and rub in lightly with the fingertips until the mixture resembles fine breadcrumbs. Season lightly and stir in the wholemeal breadcrumbs, cheese and parsley. Spoon the topping over the turkey and vegetable mixture and bake in the centre of a preheated oven, 190°C (375°F), Gas Mark 5, for 35–40 minutes or until the topping is crisp and golden brown.

2 carrots, thinly sliced

1 leek, sliced

40 g (1½ oz) butter

1 onion, finely chopped

40 g (1½ oz) plain flour

250 ml (8 fl oz) Chicken Stock (see page 8) or turkey stock

375 g (12 oz) can sweetcorn with peppers, drained and juice reserved

250 g (8 oz) cooked skinless turkey, cut into chunks

salt and pepper

Topping:

75 g (3 oz) wholemeal flour

50 g (2 oz) chilled butter

75 g (3 oz) wholemeal breadcrumbs

25 g (1 oz) Cheddar cheese, grated

1 tablespoon chopped parsley

Serves 6
Preparation time: 10–15 minutes
Cooking time: about 1¼ hours
kcal 345; kJ 1443; protein 18 g; fat 16 g; CHO 33 g

turkey crumble

stir-fried beef with crunchy vegetables

250 g (8 oz) rump steak

2 tablespoons groundnut or vegetable oil

2 garlic cloves, crushed

1 large carrot, sliced thinly on the diagonal

250 g (8 oz) cauliflower, florets separated, stalks sliced thinly on the diagonal

125 g (4 oz) green beans, sliced diagonally into 4 cm (1½ inch) lengths

½ x 160 g (5½ oz) jar yellow bean sauce

4 tablespoons water

1 tablespoon soy sauce

125 g (4 oz) bean sprouts

salt

Serves 3

Preparation time: 20 minutes, plus freezing

Cooking time: about 10 minutes

---

kcal 278; **kJ** 1163; **protein** 26 g; **fat** 12 g; **CHO** 17 g

1 Wrap the steak in clingfilm and place it in the freezer for about 1 hour or until just frozen, then cut it into thin strips across the grain, discarding any fat and sinew.

2 Heat a wok until hot. Add the oil and heat over a moderate heat until hot. Add the meat and garlic, increase the heat to high and stir-fry for about 2 minutes or until the meat is browned on all sides. Remove with a slotted spoon and set aside on a plate.

3 Add the carrot, cauliflower and beans and stir-fry for 3–4 minutes. Add the yellow bean sauce, water and soy sauce and stir-fry until well mixed. Return the meat and juices to the wok, add the bean sprouts and stir-fry for a further 2 minutes or until the flavours are blended and the mixture is hot. Add salt to taste, if necessary. Serve immediately.

1 Place the pork steaks in a large, shallow dish and pour over the orange juice. Add the juniper berries and season with salt and pepper. Cover and set aside to marinate for at least 3 hours, turning the pork from time to time.

2 Remove the pork steaks from the marinade and arrange on a grill rack. Place under a preheated moderate grill and grill for about 15 minutes or until the pork is cooked through, turning from time to time and basting frequently with the marinade.

3 Strain the remaining marinade into a saucepan. Bring to the boil and continue boiling until reduced slightly. Transfer the pork steaks to a warmed serving dish and spoon the sauce over them. Garnish with orange slices and serve immediately.

pork with juniper & orange

4 pork steaks, each about 125 g (4 oz), trimmed

300 ml (½ pint) unsweetened orange juice

12–20 juniper berries, crushed

salt and pepper

orange slices, to garnish

Serves 4

Preparation time: 10 minutes, plus marinating

Cooking time: about 20 minutes

kcal 174; kJ 730; **protein** 21 g; **fat** 7 g; **CHO** 7 g

catalan pork stew with tomatoes & aubergines

1 Heat 2 tablespoons of the oil in a large saucepan or flameproof casserole, add the pork and sauté gently until golden brown all over, turning occasionally. Remove from the pan with a slotted spoon.

2 Add the onion and garlic and cook until soft and golden. Return the meat to the pan and stir in the tomatoes, green pepper, paprika and stock. Season with salt and pepper. Bring to the boil, then lower the heat, cover the pan with greaseproof paper and a lid and simmer gently for 1 hour or until the meat is tender.

3 Dip the aubergine slices in seasoned flour. Heat some of the remaining oil in a large frying pan. When it is hot, fry the aubergine slices, a few at a time, until they are golden brown on both sides, adding more oil as required. Remove with a slotted spoon and pat dry with kitchen paper.

4 Serve the stew sprinkled with coriander, with the aubergine slices and plain boiled rice.

3 tablespoons olive oil

750 g (1½ lb) lean pork, cut into 2.5 cm (1 inch) cubes

1 large onion, sliced

2 garlic cloves, crushed

500 g (1 lb) tomatoes, skinned and chopped

1 green pepper, cored, deseeded and chopped

1½ teaspoons paprika

150 ml (¼ pint) Chicken Stock (see page 8)

salt and pepper

To Serve:

1 small aubergine, sliced

2–3 tablespoons seasoned flour

1 tablespoon chopped coriander leaves

plain boiled rice

Serves 6
Preparation time: 20 minutes
Cooking time: 1¼ hours
kcal 295; **kJ** 1255; **protein** 28 g; **fat** 15 g; **CHO** 13 g

provençal bean stew

1 Drain the beans, place them in a saucepan and cover with cold water. Bring to the boil and boil for 10 minutes, then cover and simmer for 1–1¼ hours, until almost tender, adding a pinch of salt towards the end of cooking. Drain the beans, reserving 300 ml (½ pint) of the cooking liquid.

2 Heat the oil in a pan, add the onions and fry until softened. Add the peppers and garlic and fry gently for 10 minutes. Stir in the tomatoes with their juice, tomato purée, the beans and the reserved liquid, bouquet garni and salt and pepper to taste. Cover and simmer for 45 minutes, adding the olives and parsley 5 minutes before the end of the cooking time.

3 To serve, remove the bouquet garni and transfer the stew to a warmed serving dish. Salad makes a good accompaniment.

375 g (12 oz) dried haricot beans or pinto beans, soaked overnight

2 tablespoons olive oil

2 onions, sliced

1 red pepper, cored, deseeded and sliced

1 green pepper, cored, deseeded and sliced

2 garlic cloves, crushed

400 g (13 oz) can chopped tomatoes

2 tablespoons tomato purée

1 bouquet garni

50 g (2 oz) black olives, halved and pitted

2 tablespoons chopped parsley

salt and pepper

Serves 4

Preparation time: 20 minutes, plus soaking

Cooking time: 2–2¼ hours

---

kcal 382; kJ 1617; **protein** 22 g; **fat** 9 g; **CHO** 57 g

1 tablespoon oil

1 onion, chopped

1 carrot, chopped

1 celery stick, chopped

175 g (6 oz) red split lentils

450 ml (¾ pint) water

1 garlic clove, crushed

2 tablespoons fresh wholemeal breadcrumbs

125 g (4 oz) Cheddar cheese, grated

2 tablespoons chopped parsley

1 egg, beaten

2 tablespoons sesame seeds

salt and pepper

parsley sprigs, to garnish

1 Heat the oil in a saucepan, add the onion and fry until soft. Add the carrot, celery, lentils, water, garlic and salt and pepper to taste. Cover the pan and bring to the boil, then lower the heat and simmer gently for about 20 minutes, until all the water is absorbed.

2 Add the breadcrumbs, three-quarters of the cheese, the parsley and egg to the lentil mixture and stir until thoroughly mixed. Spoon the mixture into a 1 litre (1¾ pint) shallow ovenproof dish and smooth the top.

3 Sprinkle the sesame seeds and the remaining cheese over the top then bake in a preheated oven, 180°C (350°F), Gas Mark 4, for 45 minutes, until the topping is crisp and golden brown. Serve garnished with parsley sprigs.

Serves 6

Preparation time: 10–15 minutes

Cooking time: 1¼ hours

kcal 250; **kJ** 1052; **protein** 15 g; **fat** 12 g; **CHO** 22 g

cheese & lentil gratin

banana & apricot yogurt ●

peach & passion fruit chantilly ●

strawberries with blackcurrant sauce ●

orange & lemon mousse ●

oriental fruit salad ●

gooseberry & mint sorbet ●

sicilian peach water ice ●

poached pears ●

kiwi fruit meringue cake ●

curd cheese hearts ●

griddled figs with greek yogurt & honey ●

desserts

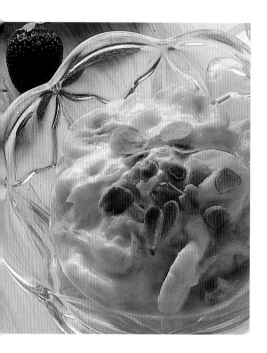

125 g (4 oz) dried apricots, chopped

300 g (10 oz) natural yogurt

1 banana

1 tablespoon flaked almonds, toasted

1 Place the apricots in a bowl with the yogurt. Mix well, then cover and leave in the refrigerator overnight.

2 Slice the banana and fold into the yogurt mixture. To serve, spoon into individual glasses and sprinkle with the almonds.

Serves 4

Preparation time: 10 minutes, plus chilling

kcal 147; **kJ** 623; **protein** 6 g; **fat** 3 g; **CHO** 25 g

banana & apricot yogurt

peach & passion fruit chantilly

1 Cut the passion fruit in half with a sharp knife, and scoop the flesh into a bowl. Slice the peaches thinly and add to the passion fruit. Carefully toss the fruit together, then spoon into 4 individual glasses or serving dishes.

2 Whip the cream with the orange flower water, if using, until it stands in soft peaks. Spoon a little cream on to each fruit salad just before serving.

3 passion fruit

6 peaches, skinned, halved and stoned

125 ml (4 fl oz) whipping cream

2 tablespoons orange flower water (optional)

| **Serves 4** |
| **Preparation time:** 10 minutes |
| kcal 170; **kJ** 713; **protein** 6 g; **fat** 3 g; **CHO** 25 g |

■ Passion fruit, which are also known as granadilla, are ready to eat when their skins are dimpled. All the flesh, including the pips, may be eaten.

1 To make the sauce, put the blackcurrants into a saucepan with the honey and red wine and stir well, then simmer gently for about 5 minutes or until the natural fruit juices are released.

2 Pour the blackcurrants and their liquid into a food processor or blender and process until fairly smooth – the sauce should still have some texture. Leave to cool.

3 Arrange the halved strawberries on a serving dish and spoon the blackcurrant sauce beside them. Decorate with the redcurrant sprigs.

250 g (8 oz) blackcurrants, trimmed

2 tablespoons clear honey

3 tablespoons red wine

375 g (12 oz) strawberries, hulled and halved

small redcurrant sprigs, to decorate

Serves 4

Preparation time: 25 minutes, plus cooling

Cooking time: 5 minutes

kcal 88; **kJ** 374; **protein** 2 g; **fat** 0 g; **CHO** 20 g

strawberries with blackcurrant sauce

1 Put the egg yolks and sugar into a bowl. Add the lemon rind and juice, orange rind and half of the orange juice.

2 Pour the remaining orange juice into a small cup and sprinkle on the gelatine. Stand the cup in a pan of hot water and stir until the gelatine has dissolved.

3 Place the bowl with the egg yolk mixture over a pan of gently simmering water and whisk until the mixture is thick and pale. Remove from the heat and continue whisking until cool. Stir the yogurt and the dissolved gelatine into the egg yolk mixture. Leave in a cool place until thick and just beginning to set.

4 Beat in the egg whites until just stiff, then fold into the mousse. Pour into a serving bowl and chill in the refrigerator for at least 2 hours before serving.

4 large eggs, separated

125 g (4 oz) light soft brown sugar

finely grated rind and juice of 2 lemons

finely grated rind and juice of 2 oranges

15 g (½ oz) gelatine

150 ml (¼ pint) natural yogurt

Serves 4

Preparation time: 30 minutes, plus cooling and chilling

Cooking time: about 10 minutes

kcal 220; kJ 934; protein 12 g; fat 6 g; CHO 33 g

orange & lemon mousse

oriental fruit salad

1 Put the sugar, star anise and cinnamon stick into a heavy-based saucepan and pour in the cold water. Heat gently until the sugar has dissolved, then boil without stirring for 2 minutes. Remove from the heat, cover and leave to cool.

2 Meanwhile, prepare the fruit. Remove the skin and eyes from the pineapple, then cut the fruit lengthways into quarters. Cut away the core, then slice the flesh crossways into bite-sized pieces. Cut the mangoes lengthways into 3, avoiding the stone. Cut a crosshatch design in the flesh of the two rounded pieces of mango, then push them inside out so that the squares stand out. Slice off the squares of flesh. Cut the remaining mango flesh from around the stone, then cut it into bite-sized pieces. Peel the lychees and remove the stones.

3 Put the fruit into a large bowl, strain the sugar syrup over it and add the rice wine or sherry. Stir gently to mix. Cover tightly and chill in the refrigerator for at least 4 hours. Before serving, decorate the fruit salad with whole star anise, physalis and pineapple leaves. To expose the orange fruit of the physalis, open the papery husks and pull them back from the fruit, turning the husks inside out. Twist the husks very tightly at the base so that they stay put.

75 g (3 oz) sugar

2 star anise

1 cinnamon stick

200 ml (7 fl oz) cold water

1 ripe pineapple

2 ripe mangoes

250 g (8 oz) lychees

4 tablespoons rice wine or dry sherry

To Decorate:

star anise

physalis (Cape gooseberries)

pineapple leaves

Serves 6

Preparation time: 30 minutes, plus chilling

Cooking time: 3–4 minutes

---

kcal 120; **kJ** 513; **protein** 1 g; **fat** 0 g; **CHO** 31 g

■ To save time, buy tubs of ready-prepared fresh pineapple and mango packed in their own natural juice. Fresh lychees are seasonal and are usually to be found in the shops around Christmas, but canned lychees are also very good.

1   Place the gooseberries in a saucepan with 1 tablespoon of the sugar, the honey and mint. Cover and simmer for 10–15 minutes until soft, then leave to cool.

2   Purée the fruit in a food processor or blender. Rub through a sieve to remove the pips. Blend the purée with the yogurt. Whisk the egg white until stiff, then gradually whisk in the remaining sugar. Fold into the fruit, then spoon the mixture into a freezerproof container. Cover and freeze for 3 hours.

3   Transfer the sorbet to the refrigerator 20–30 minutes before serving to soften a little. Scoop into glass bowls and decorate with mint sprigs.

500 g (1 lb) gooseberries

2 tablespoons soft brown sugar

1 tablespoon clear honey

8 large mint sprigs

150 g (5 oz) natural yogurt

1 egg white

mint sprigs, to decorate

Serves 4

Preparation time: 15 minutes, plus cooling and freezing

Cooking time: 10–15 minutes

kcal 113; **kJ** 479; **protein** 4 g; **fat** 1 g; **CHO** 24 g

gooseberry & mint sorbet

sicilian peach water ice

1 Put the sugar and water into a small saucepan and heat gently until the sugar has dissolved, then boil for 3–4 minutes. Set aside until cold.

2 Immerse the peaches in boiling water for 1 minute, then drain and remove the skins and stones. Purée the flesh in a food processor or blender or press through a nylon sieve. Mix the purée with the lemon juice to prevent discolouration then stir in the cold syrup. Pour into a shallow freezer tray and freeze until slushy.

3 Turn the mixture into a bowl and whisk vigorously for a few minutes, then return to the tray and freeze until firm.

4 Transfer the ice to the refrigerator 30–40 minutes before serving to allow it to soften a little. To serve, scoop it into individual glasses or bowls.

125 g (4 oz) sugar
150 ml (¼ pint) water
4 large peaches
juice of 1 lemon

Serves 4

Preparation time: 15 minutes, plus freezing

kcal 174; kJ 742; protein 2 g; fat 0 g; CHO 44 g

■ Melon ice can be made the same way by replacing the peaches in this recipe with 750 g (1½ lb) ripe, peeled and deseeded Charentais or Ogen melon flesh.

1 Put the pears into a deep ovenproof casserole just large enough to hold them standing up.

2 Put the wine, sugar and lemon rind into a small saucepan, bring to the boil and cook, stirring, until the sugar has dissolved. Pour the syrup over the pears and add enough water to come just level with the stalks. Cover the dish and bake in a preheated oven, 160°C (325°F), Gas Mark 3, for 1½ hours or until the pears are tender when tested with a fine skewer.

3 Remove the pears from the oven and leave to cool. Cover the casserole and chill, spooning the syrup over the pears from time to time.

4 Serve with sprigs of lemon balm and slivers of lemon rind.

4 pears, peeled but stalks left on

250 ml (8 fl oz) red wine

100 g (3½ oz) caster sugar

1 long sliver of lemon rind, extra for decoration

125–250 ml (4–8 fl oz) water

lemon balm sprigs, to decorate

Serves 4
Preparation time: 10–15 minutes, plus chilling
Cooking time: about 1½ hours

kcal 240; **kJ** 1020; **protein** 1 g; **fat** 0 g; **CHO** 51 g

poached pears

■ Choose firm pears, such as Williams, for this classic dessert. If necessary, trim the bases before cooking so they stand evenly in the casserole.

1 Cover a baking sheet with nonstick baking paper or foil and lightly brush with oil.

2 Half whisk the egg whites. Add the cream of tartar and whisk until very stiff. Whisk in the sugar a little at a time. Finally whisk in the cornflour.

3 Spoon the meringue mixture on to the prepared baking sheet and lightly flatten into an 18 cm (7 inch) circle with a palette knife, building up the edge of the meringue slightly.

4 Bake the meringue in a preheated oven, 110°C (225°F), Gas Mark ¼, for about 1½ hours, until set. Remove from the oven and allow to cool, then carefully peel off the lining paper.

5 Transfer the meringue to a serving plate and arrange the kiwi fruit on top. Serve on the day of making.

vegetable oil, for brushing

3 egg whites

1 teaspoon cream of tartar

75 g (3 oz) caster sugar

1 teaspoon cornflour

4 kiwi fruit, peeled and thinly sliced

Serves 4
Preparation time: 10 minutes
Cooking time: about 1½ hours

Kcal 120; kJ 506; **protein** 3 g; **fat** 0 g; **CHO** 28 g

kiwi fruit meringue cake

curd cheese hearts

1 Mix the cottage cheese with a little sweetener to taste (if you don't have a very sweet tooth, this may not be necessary). Blend in the yogurt.

2 Whisk the egg whites until stiff but not dry. Fold lightly but thoroughly into the cheese mixture, together with the brandy.

3 Line 4 small perforated heart-shaped moulds with clean muslin. Spoon the cheese mixture into the lined moulds and cover with another layer of muslin.

4 Place the moulds on a tray or baking sheet with a rim, and chill for 6–8 hours. The excess liquid should have drained away from the cheese, and the moulds should be firm enough to turn out.

5 Unmould the hearts and decorate with mint leaves and clusters of grapes.

250 g (8 oz) low-fat cottage cheese, sieved

artificial sweetener, to taste

150 ml (¼ pint) natural yogurt

2 egg whites

1 tablespoon brandy

To Decorate:

mint leaves

small clusters of black grapes

Serves 4

Preparation time: 30 minutes, plus chilling

Kcal 94; **kJ** 396; **protein** 11 g; **fat** 3 g; **CHO** 5 g

1 Heat a griddle pan and add the figs. Cook for 8 minutes, turning occasionally, until they are charred on the outside. Remove from the griddle pan and cut in half.

2 Arrange the figs on individual plates and serve with a spoonful of Greek yogurt and some honey spooned over the top.

8 ripe figs

4 tablespoons Greek yogurt

2 tablespoons clear honey

Serves 4
Preparation time: 5 minutes
Cooking time: 10 minutes
kcal 155; **kJ** 658; **protein** 4 g; **fat** 4 g; **CHO** 27 g

griddled figs with greek yogurt & honey

baking

yogurt scones

1 Sift the flour, salt and baking powder into a mixing bowl. Rub in the fat until the mixture resembles breadcrumbs, then stir in the sugar. Add the yogurt and mix to form a soft dough.

2 Turn on to a floured surface, knead lightly and roll out to a 2 cm (¾ inch) thickness. Cut into 5 cm (2 inch) rounds with a fluted cutter and place on a floured baking sheet. Brush with milk, sprinkle with sesame seeds and bake in a preheated oven, 220°C (425°F), Gas Mark 7, for 12–15 minutes. Transfer to a wire rack to cool.

250 g (8 oz) wholemeal flour, plus extra, for dusting

½ teaspoon salt

½ teaspoon baking powder

50 g (2 oz) margarine or butter

1 tablespoon muscovado or soft dark brown sugar

150 g (5 oz) natural yogurt

milk, for brushing

sesame seeds, for sprinkling

Makes 12–14
Preparation time: 15 minutes
Cooking time: 12–15 minutes

kcal 111; **kJ** 469; **protein** 3 g; **fat** 4 g; **CHO** 16 g per scone

1   Sift the flour and salt into a mixing bowl and warm gently. Rub in the fat. Blend the fresh yeast with the warm milk and leave for 10 minutes to froth. If using dried yeast, sprinkle into the milk and leave for 15–20 minutes until frothy.

2   Pour the yeast liquid into the flour and mix, adding a little more milk if necessary. Beat until the dough leaves the sides of the bowl clean, then turn on to a floured surface and knead for 10 minutes. Put the dough into an oiled polythene bag and leave to rise until doubled in bulk.

3   Knock back the dough by pushing your fist into it so that it sinks. Make a fat sausage shape and cut across into 8 equal-sized pieces. Shape into rounds or ovals. Press down firmly with the heel of your hand and release. Place the rolls on a floured baking sheet, leaving room for expansion. Cover and leave to rise for 15 minutes or until doubled in size.

4   Dust the rolls with flour and bake in the centre of a preheated oven, 230°C (450°), Gas Mark 8, for 15–20 minutes. When cooked, remove to a wire rack and cover with a tea towel.

soft wholemeal rolls

250 g (8 oz) wholemeal flour, plus extra for dusting

1 teaspoon salt

25 g (1 oz) margarine

15 g (½ oz) fresh yeast or
1½ teaspoons dried yeast with
1 teaspoon sugar

about 150 ml (¼ pint) warm milk

Makes 8

Preparation time: 25 minutes, plus dissolving the yeast, rising and proving

---

Cooking time: 15–20 minutes

---

kcal 130; **kJ** 548; **protein** 5; **fat** 4 g; **CHO** 21 g per roll

bread pudding

1 Place the bread in a large bowl, cover with cold water and leave to soak for about 20 minutes.

2 Drain the bread and squeeze it to remove as much water as possible. Return to the bowl and beat well with a fork. Stir in the fruit, mixed peel, brown sugar and mixed spice.

3 Place the butter and marmalade in a pan and heat gently until melted. Take care not to overheat. Pour the butter and marmalade on to the eggs, mix well and stir into the bread mixture. Pour into a buttered ovenproof dish, sprinkle with the caster sugar and bake in a preheated oven, 160°C (325°F), Gas Mark 3, for 1½–1¾ hours until golden brown and firm. Serve hot or cold cut into slices.

250 g (8 oz) stale bread, cut into chunks

250 g (8 oz) dried mixed fruit

50 g (2 oz) mixed peel (optional)

75 g (3 oz) soft brown sugar

¼ teaspoon mixed spice

50 g (2 oz) unsalted butter

2 tablespoons marmalade

2 eggs, beaten

1–2 tablespoons caster sugar

Serves 6
Preparation time: 15 minutes, plus soaking
Cooking time: 1½–1¾ hours
kcal 385 kJ; 1628; **protein** 6 g; **fat** 10 g; **CHO** 73 g

■ Although this pudding is usually made with white bread, it is equally delicious made with brown or wholemeal bread.

banana & walnut slices

1 Cream the fat and sugar in a mixing bowl until light and fluffy. Beat in the eggs, one at a time, adding 1 tablespoon of flour with the second egg. Fold in the remaining flour, baking powder and bananas.

2 Spread the mixture evenly in a lined and greased 20 cm (8 inch) square shallow tin. Sprinkle with the walnuts and bake in a preheated oven, 190°C (375°F), Gas Mark 5, for 20–25 minutes until the cake springs back when lightly pressed.

3 Leave in the tin for 2 minutes, then cut into 16 slices. Transfer to a wire rack to cool.

125 g (4 oz) margarine or butter

125 g (4 oz) sugar

2 eggs

125 g (4 oz) wholemeal flour

2 teaspoons baking powder

2 bananas, mashed

125 g (4 oz) walnuts, chopped

Makes 16 slices
Preparation time: 15 minutes
Cooking time: 20–25 minutes

kcal 188; **kJ** 785; **protein** 3 g; **fat** 13 g; **CHO** 17 g per slice

1 Spread the sesame seeds in a shallow tin and bake in a preheated oven, 160°C (325°F), Gas Mark 3, stirring occasionally, for 6–8 minutes, or until lightly toasted. Set aside, leaving the oven on.

2 Sift the flour, baking powder and salt into a bowl, then set aside.

3 Cream the butter or margarine and brown sugar in a bowl until light and fluffy. Beat in the egg. Add the vanilla and mix well. Gradually add the flour mixture until just blended. Add the toasted sesame seeds and stir until well combined.

4 Place rounded teaspoonfuls about 5 cm (2 inches) apart on greased baking sheets. Bake in the oven for 9–10 minutes or until the biscuits are lightly browned. They are very fragile when they first come out of the oven so leave them on the baking sheets to cool for about 1 minute, then carefully transfer to wire racks to cool completely.

50 g (2 oz) sesame seeds

65 g (2½ oz) plain flour

¼ teaspoon baking powder

⅛ teaspoon salt

125 g (4 oz) butter or margarine, softened

125 g (4 oz) soft brown sugar

1 egg

1 teaspoon vanilla essence

Makes about 48

Preparation time: 20 minutes

Cooking time: 15–18 minutes

kcal 42; kJ 174; protein 1 g; fat 3 g; CHO 4 g per wafer

vanilla & sesame wafers

index